Robert Rose's

Muffins
Cookies
& MORE

TUPPERWARE
EDITION

Robert Rose's Muffins, Cookies & More

DESIGN, EDITORIAL & PRODUCTION: MATTHEWS COMMUNICATIONS DESIGN INC.
COLOR SCANS & FILM: POINTONE GRAPHICS
INDEXER: BARBARA SCHON

COVER PHOTO: BANANA PEANUT BUTTER CHIP MUFFINS (PAGE 6)

Canadian Cataloguing in Publication Data

Main entry under title:

Muffins, cookies & more

ISBN 0-7788-0011-3

1. Muffins. 2. Cookies. I. Title: Muffins, cookies and more.

TX770.M83M83 1999   641.8'15   C99-930131-4

Published by: Robert Rose Inc. • 156 Duncan Mill Road, Suite 12 Toronto, Ontario, Canada M3B 2N2   Tel: (416) 449-3535
Printed in Canada
1234567 BP 02 01 00 99

This book contains recipes specially selected from a number of full-sized cookbooks published by Robert Rose Inc., including: *The Comfort Food Cookbook* and *Fast & Easy Cooking*, both by Johanna Burkhard; Rose Reisman's *Light Cooking, Enlightened Home Cooking*, and *Light Vegetarian Cooking*; and, *The Robert Rose Book of Classic Desserts*.

CONTENTS

MUFFINS

Banana Peanut Butter Chip Muffins   6

Carrot-Raisin Muffins   7

Blueberry Cornmeal Muffins   8

Banana Spice Muffins   9

Bran Muffins   10

COOKIES

No-Fail Shortbread   12

Lemon Sugar Cookies   15

Gingersnaps   16

Peanut Butter-Coconut-Raisin Granola Bars   18

Peanut Butter Chocolate Chip Cookies   20

Oatmeal Date Cookies   21

Double Chocolate Chunk Cookies   23

Pecan Biscotti   24

CAKES AND CHEESECAKES

Strawberry Cream Cake   27

Apple Pecan Streusel Cake   29

Carrot Cake with Cream Cheese Frosting   30

Chocolate Cheesecake with Sour Cream Topping   33

Marble Mocha Cheesecake   34

Glazed Espresso Chocolate Cake   36

PIES, TARTS AND OTHER DESSERTS

Strawberry Kiwi Cream Cheese Chocolate Flan   38

Cream Cheese-Filled Brownies   41

Lemon and Lime Meringue Pie   42

Chocolate Pecan Pie   44

Tropical Fruit Tart   46

Muffins

Banana Chocolate Chip Muffins

MAKES 12 MUFFINS

PREHEAT OVEN TO 375° F (190° C)
12 MUFFIN CUPS SPRAYED WITH VEGETABLE SPRAY

Make Ahead: Prepare up to a day ahead. These freeze well up to 4 weeks.

2/3 cup	granulated sugar	150 mL
3 tbsp	vegetable oil	45 mL
3 tbsp	peanut butter	45 mL
1	large banana, mashed	1
1	egg	1
1 tsp	vanilla	5 mL
3/4 cup	all-purpose flour	175 mL
3/4 tsp	baking powder	4 mL
3/4 tsp	baking soda	4 mL
1/4 cup	2% yogurt	50 mL
3 tbsp	semi-sweet chocolate chips	45 mL

1. In a Thatsa® Bowl, combine sugar, oil, peanut butter, banana, egg and vanilla; mix using a Tupperific spatula until well blended. In a Thatsa® Bowl Jr., combine flour, baking powder and baking soda; add to batter and mix just until blended. Stir in yogurt and chocolate chips.

2. Fill muffin cups half-full. Bake 15 to 18 minutes, or until tops are firm to the touch and cake tester inserted in the center comes out dry.

Carrot-Raisin Muffins

MAKES 16 LARGE MUFFINS

PREHEAT OVEN TO 375° F (190° C)

Packed with nuts, fruits and carrots, these scrumptious muffins are perfect for breakfast. But they are just as tasty for afternoon snacks.

2 cups	all-purpose flour	500 mL
3/4 cup	granulated sugar	175 mL
1 1/2 tsp	cinnamon	7 mL
1 tsp	baking powder	5 mL
1 tsp	baking soda	5 mL
1/2 tsp	ground nutmeg	2 mL
1/2 tsp	salt	2 mL
1 1/2 cups	grated carrots (about 3 medium)	375 mL
1 cup	grated peeled apples	250 mL
1/2 cup	raisins	125 mL
1/2 cup	shredded sweetened coconut	125 mL
1/2 cup	chopped walnuts (optional)	125 mL
2	large eggs	2
2/3 cup	plain yogurt	150 mL
1/3 cup	vegetable oil	75 mL

1. In a Thatsa® Bowl, stir together flour, sugar, cinnamon, baking powder, baking soda, nutmeg and salt. Using a Tupperific spatula, stir in carrots, apples, raisins, coconut and walnuts.

2. In a Thatsa® Bowl Jr., beat eggs; add yogurt and oil. Stir into flour mixture just until combined. (Batter will be very thick.)

3. Spoon batter into well-greased or paper-lined muffins cups filling almost to the top.

4. Bake in preheated oven for 25 to 30 minutes or until tops spring back when lightly touched. Let cool in pans for 5 minutes; transfer muffins to Tupperware® Cupcake Taker.

Blueberry Cornmeal Muffins

MAKES 12 MUFFINS

PREHEAT OVEN TO 400° F (200° C)

When it comes to celebrating the pleasure of summer fruits, nothing beats juicy blueberries. They are especially welcome when teamed with lemon.

To minimize the problem of frozen blueberries tinting the batter blue, place berries in a double colander and quickly rinse under cold water to get rid of any ice crystals. Blot dry with paper towels. Place berries in a Thatsa® Bowl Mini and toss with 2 tbsp (25 mL) of the muffin flour mixture. Use immediately; fold into batter with a few quick strokes. Measure all ingredients into Modern Measuring Cups.

1 1/2 cups	all-purpose flour	375 mL
1/3 cup	cornmeal	75 mL
1/2 cup	granulated sugar	125 mL
2 1/2 tsp	baking powder	12 mL
1/4 tsp	salt	1 mL
1	large egg	1
3/4 cup	milk	175 mL
1/4 cup	butter, melted	50 mL
1 tsp	grated lemon rind	5 mL
1 cup	fresh or frozen blueberries	250 mL

1. In a Thatsa® Bowl stir together flour, cornmeal, sugar, baking powder and salt.

2. In a Thatsa® Bowl Jr., beat egg; stir in milk, melted butter and lemon rind. Combine with dry ingredients until just mixed. Gently fold in blueberries.

3. Spoon into greased or paper-lined muffin cups so they are three-quarters full. Bake in pre-heated oven for 20 to 24 minutes or until top is firm to the touch and lightly browned. Remove from pans and let muffins cool.

Banana Spice Muffins

MAKES 12 MUFFINS

PREHEAT OVEN TO 400° F (200° C)
MUFFIN PAN WITH PAPER LINERS

*Whip up this batch of muffins and they'll be gone in no time.
They are especially child-friendly, but they'll also be enjoyed by the
adults in the house.*

*Don't overmix the batter.
Use quick gentle strokes to combine the dry and liquid ingredients
together. It's normal to have a few lumps
remaining in the batter.*

1	large egg	1
1 cup	mashed ripe bananas (about 3)	250 mL
3/4 cup	packed brown sugar	175 mL
1/2 cup	plain low-fat yogurt	125 mL
1/4 cup	vegetable oil	50 mL
2 cups	all-purpose flour	500 mL
1 1/2 tsp	baking powder	7 mL
1 1/2 tsp	cinnamon	7 mL
1/2 tsp	baking soda	2 mL
1/2 tsp	ground nutmeg	2 mL
1/4 tsp	ground cloves	1 mL
1/4 tsp	salt	1 mL
1/2 cup	raisins	125 mL

1. In a Thatsa® Bowl, beat egg; stir in bananas, brown sugar, yogurt and oil until smooth. In another bowl, combine flour, baking powder, cinnamon, baking soda, nutmeg, cloves and salt; stir into banana mixture until just combined. Fold in raisins with a Tupperific Spatula.

2. Spoon batter into paper-lined muffin cups until level with top of pan. Bake for 20 to 25 minutes or until top springs back when lightly touched. Transfer muffins to a rack and let cool.

Bran Muffins

MAKES 12 MUFFINS

PREHEAT OVEN TO 400° F (200° C)

Bran muffins are never out of style. Nicely moistened with molasses, these muffins will become a morning favorite.

Always measure the oil before measuring sticky sweeteners like molasses and honey. (For recipes that don't call for oil, spray measure with nonstick vegetable spray or lightly coat with oil. You'll find every last drop of sweetener will easily pour out.)

2	large eggs	2
1 cup	buttermilk	250 mL
1/3 cup	packed brown sugar	75 mL
1/4 cup	vegetable oil	50 mL
1/4 cup	molasses	50 mL
1 1/4 cups	whole-wheat flour	300 mL
1 cup	natural bran	250 mL
1 tsp	baking soda	5 mL
1/2 tsp	baking powder	2 mL
1/4 tsp	salt	1 mL
1/2 cup	raisins or chopped apricots	125 mL

1. In a Thatsa® Bowl, beat eggs; add buttermilk, brown sugar, oil and molasses.

2. In a separate bowl, combine flour, bran, baking soda, baking powder and salt. Stir into liquid ingredients to make a smooth batter; fold in raisins.

3. Spoon into greased or paper-lined muffin cups so they are three-quarters full. Bake in pre-heated oven for 20 to 24 minutes or until tops spring back when lightly touched. Let cool 10 minutes; remove from pan and cool on racks.

Cookies

No-Fail Shortbread

MAKES ABOUT 4 DOZEN COOKIES

PREHEAT OVEN TO 300° F (150° C)

The secret to this tender shortbread is not to overwork the dough.

1 cup	unsalted butter, softened	250 mL
1/2 cup	superfine sugar (fruit sugar)	125 mL
1 tsp	vanilla	5 mL
2 cups	sifted all-purpose flour	500 mL
1/4 tsp	salt	1 mL

1. In a Thatsa® Bowl, beat butter with a Tupperific Spatula until fluffy; beat in sugar a spoonful at time until well blended. Beat in vanilla. Stir in flour and salt; shape dough into a ball. On a lightly floured board, gently knead 4 to 5 times or until smooth.

2. Divide dough into 4 pieces. Using a Tupperware® Rolling Pin roll each out on lightly floured Pastry Sheet to 1/3-inch (8 mm) thickness; cut out shapes using cookie cutters. Place on ungreased baking sheets. Bake, one sheet at a time, in middle of preheated oven for 25 to 30 minutes or until edges are light golden.

Lemon Sugar Cookies

MAKES ABOUT 6 DOZEN COOKIES
PREHEAT OVEN TO 350° F (180° C)

1 cup	unsalted butter, softened	250 mL
1 1/4 cups	granulated sugar	300 mL
2	whole eggs	2
1	egg yolk	1
1 tbsp	grated lemon rind	15 mL
3 cups	all-purpose flour	750 mL
1/2 tsp	baking powder	2 mL
1/2 tsp	salt	2 mL
1	egg white, lightly beaten	1
	Granulated sugar	

1. In a Batter Bowl using an electric mixer, cream butter and sugar until light and fluffy. Beat in eggs, egg yolk and lemon rind until incorporated. In a Thatsa® Bowl Jr., combine flour, baking powder and salt; stir into butter mixture to make a smooth dough. Seal and refrigerate for 4 hours or overnight. (Dough can also be frozen for up to 1 month.)

2. Divide dough in half. On the Pastry Sheet, roll each piece out to a scant 1/4-inch (5 mm) thickness. Cut out shapes using assorted cookie cutters; place on greased baking sheets. Lightly brush with egg white; using a small spoon, sprinkle tops with a light coating of granulated sugar. Bake, one sheet at a time, in the middle of preheated oven for 12 to 14 minutes or until light golden around edges. Remove cookies to a rack to cool.

Gingersnaps

MAKES ABOUT 5 DOZEN COOKIES

PREHEAT OVEN TO 350° F (180° C)
BAKING SHEET(S), LIGHTLY GREASED

A favorite since my university days, these spice cookies would provide fuel for cram sessions before exams. Now, continuing the tradition, I bake a batch when my kids have to hit the books.

Be sure to use fresh baking soda as it makes cookies crisp and light. Like baking powder, an open box of baking soda has a shelf life of only 6 months, so make sure to replenish both regularly. As a reminder, write the date when they need to be replaced on the container.

1/2 cup	shortening, softened	125 mL
1/2 cup	butter, softened	125 mL
3/4 cup	packed brown sugar	175 mL
1/4 cup	molasses	50 mL
1	large egg, beaten	1
2 1/4 cups	all-purpose flour	550 mL
1 1/2 tsp	baking soda	7 mL
1 1/2 tsp	ground ginger	7 mL
1 tsp	ground cinnamon	5 mL
1 tsp	ground cloves	5 mL
1/4 tsp	salt	1 mL
	Granulated sugar	

1. In a Thatsa® Bowl, cream shortening and butter with sugar until light and fluffy; beat in molasses and egg until creamy.

2. In a Thatsa® Bowl Jr., sift together flour, baking soda, ginger, cinnamon, ground cloves and salt. Stir into creamed mixture to make a soft dough. Refrigerate for 1 hour or until firm.

3. Shape dough into 1-inch (2.5 cm) balls; roll in bowl of granulated sugar. Arrange 2 inches (5 cm) apart on prepared baking sheets. Flatten to 1/4 inch (5 mm) thickness.

4. Bake in preheated oven for 12 to 14 minutes or until golden. Cool 2 minutes on baking sheets; transfer to rack and let cool.

Peanut Butter-Coconut-Raisin Granola Bars

MAKES 25 BARS

PREHEAT OVEN TO 350° F (180° C)
9-INCH SQUARE (2.5 L) PAN SPRAYED WITH VEGETABLE SPRAY

Corn flakes can replace bran flakes. Don't worry if you only have Raisin Bran on hand. Chopped dates can replace raisins. Use a natural smooth or chunky peanut butter. Do not overcook the peanut butter mixture.

Make Ahead: Prepare these up to 2 days ahead and keep tightly closed in a One Touch® Reminder Canister. These freeze for up to 2 weeks.

1 1/3 cups	rolled oats	325 mL
2/3 cup	raisins	150 mL
1/2 cup	bran flakes	125 mL
1/3 cup	unsweetened coconut	75 mL
3 tbsp	chocolate chips	45 mL
2 tbsp	chopped pecans	25 mL
1 tsp	baking soda	5 mL
1/4 cup	peanut butter	50 mL
1/4 cup	brown sugar	50 mL
3 tbsp	margarine or butter	45 mL
3 tbsp	honey	45 mL
1 tsp	vanilla	5 mL

1. Put oats, raisins, bran flakes, coconut, chocolate chips, pecans and baking soda in a Thatsa® Bowl. Combine until well mixed.

2. In a small saucepan, whisk together peanut butter, brown sugar, margarine, honey and vanilla over medium heat for approximately 30 seconds or just until sugar dissolves and mixture is smooth. Pour over dry ingredients and stir to combine. Press into prepared pan and bake for 15 to 20 minutes or until browned. Let cool completely before cutting into bars.

Peanut Butter Chocolate Chip Cookies

MAKES 40 COOKIES

PREHEAT OVEN TO 350° F (180° C)
BAKING SHEETS SPRAYED WITH VEGETABLE SPRAY

The longer they bake, the crisper the cookies. Nuts can replace the raisins. Use natural peanut butter made from only peanuts.

Make Ahead:Dough can be frozen up to 2 weeks. Bake just before eating for best flavor.

1/2 cup	brown sugar	125 mL
1/3 cup	granulated sugar	75 mL
1/3 cup	peanut butter	75 mL
1/3 cup	2% milk	75 mL
1/4 cup	soft margarine	50 mL
1	egg	1
1 tsp	vanilla	5 mL
1/2 cup	all-purpose flour	125 mL
1/3 cup	whole wheat flour	75 mL
1 tsp	baking soda	5 mL
1/3 cup	chocolate chips	75 mL
1/4 cup	raisins	50 mL

1. In a Batter Bowl, beat together brown and granulated sugars, peanut butter, milk, margarine, egg and vanilla until well blended.

2. In a Thatsa® Bowl, combine all-purpose and whole wheat flours and baking soda; add to the Batter Bowl and mix just until incorporated. Do not over-mix. Using a Tupperific Spatula stir in chocolate chips and raisins.

3. Drop by heaping teaspoon-fuls (5 mL) 2 inches (5 cm) apart onto baking sheets. Bake for 12 to 15 minutes or until browned.

Oatmeal Date Cookies

MAKES 32 COOKIES

PREHEAT OVEN TO 350° F (180° C)
BAKING SHEETS SPRAYED WITH VEGETABLE SPRAY

You can use Raisin Bran cereal. Do not use All-Bran or raw bran.
Replace dates with dried apricots, prunes or raisins. Chop dried fruit
with kitchen scissors. Keep dried fruits in freezer for maximum freshness.

Make Ahead: Bake cookies up to a day ahead for best flavor, keeping in a
One Touch® Reminder Canister. Freeze cookie dough for up to 2 weeks.

1/3 cup	margarine or butter	75 mL
1/3 cup	granulated sugar	75 mL
1	egg	1
1 tsp	vanilla	5 mL
2/3 cup	all-purpose flour	150 mL
1 tsp	baking powder	5 mL
3/4 tsp	cinnamon	4 mL
3/4 cup	rolled oats	175 mL
3/4 cup	bran flakes cereal or corn flakes	175 mL
2/3 cup	chopped pitted dried dates	150 mL

1. In a Thatsa® Bowl, cream together margarine and sugar. Add egg and vanilla; mix well.

2. In a Thatsa® Bowl Jr., combine flour, baking powder, cinnamon, rolled oats, cereal and dates. Add to sugar mixture and mix until just combined.

3. Drop by heaping teaspoonfuls (5 mL) onto prepared baking sheets 2 inches (5 cm) apart and press down with back of fork; bake for approximately 10 minutes or until browned.

Double Chocolate Chunk Cookies

MAKES 3 1/2 DOZEN COOKIES

PREHEAT OVEN TO 350° F (180° C)

Flecked with white chocolate chunks and walnuts, these fudgy cookies are a favorite with my family. Served with a cold glass of milk, they're pure heaven.

For perfectly baked cookies, place baking sheet on middle rack of oven; do only one sheet at time. Wipe baking sheets with paper towels or a damp cloth to remove grease. Let sheets cool completely before using again to prevent dough from spreading out too much during baking.

3/4 cup	butter, softened	175 mL
3/4 cup	granulated sugar	175 mL
1/2 cup	packed brown sugar	125 mL
2	large eggs	2
2 tsp	vanilla	10 mL
1 1/2 cups	all-purpose flour	375 mL
1/2 cup	cocoa powder	125 mL
1/2 tsp	baking soda	2 mL
1/2 tsp	salt	2 mL
1 1/2 cups	white chocolate chunks	375 mL
1 cup	chopped walnuts or pecans	250 mL

1. In a Batter bowl using an electric mixer, cream butter with granulated and brown sugars until fluffy; beat in eggs and vanilla until smooth.

2. In a Thatsa® Bowl Jr., sift together flour, cocoa powder, baking soda and salt. Beat into creamed mixture until combined; stir in white chocolate chunks and walnuts.

3. Drop tablespoonfuls (15 mL) of dough 2 inches (5 cm) apart on ungreased baking sheets.

4. Bake in preheated oven for 10 to 12 minutes or until edges are firm. (Bake for the shorter time if you prefer cookies with a soft, chewy center.) Cool 2 minutes on baking sheets; remove to wire rack and cool completely.

Pecan Biscotti

MAKES 45 COOKIES

PREHEAT OVEN TO 350° F (180° C)
BAKING SHEET SPRAYED WITH VEGETABLE SPRAY

Use almonds, hazelnuts, pine nuts or a combination.

*Make Ahead: Store in a One Touch® Reminder Canister up to 2 weeks,
or freeze for up to 1 month.*

2	eggs	2
3/4 cup	granulated sugar	175 mL
1/3 cup	margarine	75 mL
1/4 cup	water	50 mL
2 tsp	vanilla	10 mL
1 tsp	almond extract	5 mL
2 3/4 cups	all-purpose flour	675 mL
1/2 cup	chopped pecans	125 mL
2 1/4 tsp	baking powder	11 mL

1. In a Thatsa® bowl, blend eggs with sugar; beat in margarine, water, vanilla and almond extract until smooth.

2. Add flour, pecans and baking powder; mix until dough forms ball. Divide dough in half; shape each portion into a log 12 inches (30 cm) long and place on baking sheet. Bake for 20 minutes. Let cool for 5 minutes.

3. Cut logs diagonally into 1/2-inch (1 cm) thick slices. Place slices on sides on baking sheet; bake for 20 minutes or until lightly browned.

Cakes and Cheesecakes

Strawberry Cream Cake

SERVES 8 TO 10

PREHEAT OVEN TO 350° F (180° C)
9-INCH (23 CM) SPRINGFORM PAN, GREASED AND FLOURED

Nothing is more seductive than crimson strawberries, cold whipped cream and buttery-lemon cake. For me, this perfect summer dessert beats out shortcake hands down as the ultimate strawberry creation.

Strawberries can be replaced with other small fruits such as raspberries, blueberries or blackberries. Or use a combination of several berries.

For fluffy whipped cream, make sure the cream is very cold before beating. As well, place the beaters and bowl in the freezer for 10 minutes before you start.

Sponge Cake

3	large eggs	3
1 cup	granulated sugar	250 mL
1 1/2 cups	all-purpose flour	375 mL
2 tsp	baking powder	10 mL
1/4 tsp	salt	1 mL
3/4 cup	milk	175 mL
1/3 cup	butter, melted	75 mL
1 tsp	grated lemon zest	5 mL

Filling

1 1/2 cups	whipping (35%) cream	375 mL
1 tsp	vanilla	5 mL
1/4 cup	superfine sugar	50 mL
3 cups	sliced strawberries	750 mL
1 cup	whole small strawberries	250 mL
	Mint sprigs	

Recipe continues, next page ...

1. In a Batter Bowl using an electric mixer at high speed, beat eggs and sugar for 3 minutes or until thick and creamy.

2. In a Thatsa® Bowl Jr., combine flour, baking powder and salt. In a Thatsa® Bowl Mini, combine milk, melted butter and lemon zest.

3. Beat dry ingredients into egg mixture alternately with milk mixture until batter is just smooth.

4. Pour into prepared pan. Bake in preheated oven for 35 minutes or until cake tester inserted in center comes out clean.

5. Let cake cool for 5 minutes; run knife around edge and remove sides. Place on rack to cool completely. Using a long serrated knife, slice cake horizontally to make 3 layers each about 1/2 inch (1 cm) thick.

6. In a Mix-N-Stor® Plus Pitcher with an electric mixer, whip cream until soft peaks form. Beat in vanilla and sugar, a spoonful (5 mL) at a time, until stiff peaks form.

7. Arrange 1 cake layer, cut-side up on a large serving plate. Using a Sandwich Spreader, spread with one-third of the whipped cream; top with half the sliced berries, including some juice. Arrange second cake layer on top. Spread with one-third of the whipped cream and remaining sliced berries with juice. Arrange third layer on top; spread top with remaining whipped cream. Garnish with small whole berries and mint sprigs.

Apple Pecan Streusel Cake

SERVES 16

PREHEAT OVEN TO 350° F (180° C)
9-INCH (3 L) BUNDT PAN SPRAYED WITH VEGETABLE SPRAY

1/4 cup	soft margarine	50 mL
1 cup	brown sugar	250 mL
2	eggs	2
2 tsp	vanilla	10 mL
1 1/4 cups	all-purpose flour	300 mL
3/4 cup	whole wheat flour	175 mL
2 1/2 tsp	cinnamon	12 mL
1 1/2 tsp	baking powder	7 mL
1 tsp	baking soda	5 mL
1 cup	2% yogurt or light sour cream	250 mL
2 3/4 cups	diced peeled apples	675 mL
1/4 cup	raisins	50 mL

Topping

1/4 cup	chopped pecans	50 mL
1/4 cup	all-purpose flour	50 mL
3 tbsp	brown sugar	45 mL
1 tbsp	margarine, melted	15 mL
1 1/2 tsp	cinnamon	7 mL

1. Topping: In a Thatsa® Bowl Mini, combine pecans, flour, sugar, margarine and cinnamon until crumbly. Set aside.

2. In a Thatsa® Bowl, cream together margarine and sugar. Beat in eggs and vanilla until well blended.

3. Combine all-purpose and whole wheat flours, cinnamon, baking powder and baking soda; add to bowl alternately with yogurt, mixing just until blended. Fold in apples and raisins. Pour into pan.

4. Sprinkle with topping; bake for 40 to 45 minutes or until cake tester inserted into center comes out clean.

Carrot Cake with Cream Cheese Frosting

SERVES 16

PREHEAT OVEN TO 350° F (180° C)
9-INCH (3 L) BUNDT PAN SPRAYED WITH VEGETABLE SPRAY

Very ripe bananas can be kept frozen for up to 1 year.
Raisins can be replaced with chopped pitted dates, apricots or prunes.

Make Ahead: Bake up to 2 days ahead. Freeze for up to 6 weeks.

1/3 cup	margarine or butter	75 mL
1 cup	granulated sugar	250 mL
2	eggs	2
1 tsp	vanilla	5 mL
1	large ripe banana, mashed	1
2 cups	grated carrots	500 mL
2/3 cup	raisins	150 mL
1/2 cup	canned pineapple, drained and crushed	125 mL
1/2 cup	2% yogurt	125 mL
2 cups	all-purpose flour	500 mL
1 1/2 tsp	baking powder	7 mL
1 1/2 tsp	baking soda	7 mL
1 1/2 tsp	cinnamon	7 mL
1/4 tsp	nutmeg	1 mL

Icing

1/3 cup	light cream cheese, softened	75 mL
2/3 cup	icing sugar	150 mL
1 tbsp	2% milk	15 mL

1. In a Thatsa® Bowl, cream together margarine and sugar until smooth; add eggs and vanilla and beat well (mixture may look curdled). Add mashed banana, carrots, raisins, pineapple and yogurt; stir until well combined.

2. In a Thatsa® Bowl Jr. stir together flour, baking powder, baking soda, cinnamon and nutmeg. Add to the carrot mixture; stir just until combined. Pour into prepared pan and bake for 40 to 45 minutes or until cake tester inserted in the center comes out clean. Let cool for 10 minutes before inverting onto serving plate.

3. In a Mix-N-Stor® Plus Pitcher, beat together cream cheese, icing sugar and milk until smooth; drizzle over top of cake. Decorate with grated carrots if desired.

Chocolate Cheesecake with Sour Cream Topping

SERVES 12

PREHEAT OVEN TO 350° F (180° C)
8-INCH (2 L) SPRINGFORM PAN SPRAYED WITH VEGETABLE SPRAY

8 oz	ricotta cheese	250 g
8 oz	2% cottage cheese	250 g
1 cup	granulated sugar	250 mL
1	large egg	1
1 tsp	vanilla	5 mL
1/4 cup	sifted unsweetened cocoa powder	50 mL
1 tbsp	all-purpose flour	15 mL
Crust		
1 1/2 cups	graham or chocolate wafer crumbs	375 mL
2 tbsp	water	25 mL
1 tbsp	margarine, melted	15 mL
Topping		
1 cup	light sour cream	250 mL
2 tbsp	granulated sugar	25 mL
1 tsp	vanilla	5 mL

1. Crust: In a Thatsa® Bowl Jr., combine crumbs, water and margarine; mix well. Pat onto bottom and sides of springform pan. Refrigerate.

2. In a Batter Bowl, combine ricotta and cottage cheeses, sugar, egg and vanilla; process until smooth. Add cocoa and flour; beat just until combined. Pour into pan and bake for 30 minutes or until set around edge but still slightly loose in center.

3. Topping: Meanwhile, stir together sour cream, sugar and vanilla; pour over cheesecake. Bake for 10 more minutes. (Topping will be loose.) Let cool and refrigerate for at least 3 hours or until set.

Marble Mocha Cheesecake

SERVES 12

PREHEAT OVEN TO 350° F (180° C)

8-INCH (2 L) SPRINGFORM PAN SPRAYED WITH VEGETABLE SPRAY

Crust

1 1/2 cups	chocolate wafer crumbs	375 mL
2 tbsp	granulated sugar	25 mL
2 tbsp	water	25 mL
1 tbsp	margarine or butter	15 mL

Filling

1 2/3 cups	5% ricotta cheese	400 mL
1/3 cup	softened light cream cheese	75 mL
3/4 cup	granulated sugar	175 mL
1	egg	1
1/3 cup	light sour cream or 2% yogurt	75 mL
1 tbsp	all-purpose flour	15 mL
1 tsp	vanilla	5 mL
1 1/2 tsp	instant coffee granules	7 mL
1 1/2 tsp	hot water	7 mL
3 tbsp	semi-soft chocolate chips, melted	45 mL

1. Combine chocolate crumbs, sugar, water and margarine; mix thoroughly. Press into bottom and up sides of springform pan.

2. In a Batter Bowl, beat together ricotta cheese, cream cheese, sugar, egg, sour cream, flour and vanilla until well blended. Dissolve coffee granules in hot water; add to batter and mix until incorporated.

3. Pour batter into springform pan and smooth top. Drizzle melted chocolate on top. Draw a Sandwich Spreader through the chocolate and batter several times to create marbling. Bake for 35 to 40 minutes; center will be slightly loose. Let cool, and refrigerate several hours before serving.

Glazed Espresso Chocolate Cake

SERVES 16

PREHEAT OVEN TO 350° F (180° C)
8-INCH (2 L) SPRINGFORM PAN SPRAYED WITH VEGETABLE SPRAY

1/2 cup	brown sugar	125 mL
1/2 cup	granulated sugar	125 mL
1/3 cup	margarine	75 mL
2	eggs	2
1 tsp	vanilla	5 mL
1/4 cup	unsweetened cocoa powder	50 mL
1 cup	all-purpose flour	250 mL
1 tsp	baking soda	5 mL
1 tsp	baking powder	5 mL
1/2 cup	hot strong coffee	125 mL
1/3 cup	low-fat yogurt or buttermilk	75 mL
Glaze		
1 cup	icing sugar	250 mL
2 tbsp	strong coffee	25 mL
	Unsweetened cocoa powder	

1. In a Batter Bowl, beat together brown and granulated sugars, margarine, eggs and vanilla until well blended. Add cocoa and mix until well incorporated.

2. Combine flour, baking soda and baking powder; add to bowl along with coffee and yogurt. Using a Tupperific Spatula, mix just until combined, being careful not to overmix. Pour into pan; bake for 35 to 40 minutes or until tester inserted into center comes out dry. Let cool completely.

3. Glaze: In a Thatsa® Bowl Jr., mix icing sugar with coffee until smooth, adding more coffee if too thick. Spread over cake, smoothing with knife. Sift cocoa over top to decorate.

Pies, Tarts and Other Desserts

Strawberry Kiwi Cream Cheese Chocolate Flan

SERVES 8

PREHEAT OVEN TO 375° F (190° C)
9- TO 10-INCH (23 TO 25 CM) FLAN PAN WITH REMOVABLE BOTTOM

Pastry

1 1/2 cups	all-purpose flour	375 mL
1/4 cup	granulated sugar	50 mL
3/4 cup	butter	175 mL
1 1/2 tsp	white vinegar	7 mL

Filling

2 oz	semi-sweet chocolate	60 g
1 tbsp	whipping (35%) cream	15 mL
8 oz	cream cheese	250 g
3 tbsp	icing sugar	45 mL
2 tbsp	milk	25 mL
1/4 tsp	vanilla extract	1 mL

Topping

2 cups	strawberries, halved	500 mL
2	kiwi fruit, peeled and sliced	2
2 tbsp	red currant or apple jelly	25 mL
	Toasted sliced almonds	
	Icing sugar	

1. Make the pastry: In a Thatsa® Bowl Jr. stir together flour and sugar. With a pastry cutter or two knives, cut in butter to achieve a coarse crumb consistency. Sprinkle in vinegar, tossing with a fork. Form into a ball, put in a Thatsa® Bowl Jr., seal and chill 30 minutes. Pat into bottom and sides of flan pan. Freeze 5 to 10 minutes. Bake 15 to 20 minutes or until golden. Cool on wire rack.

2. Make the filling: In a bowl, melt the chocolate over hot (not boiling) water, stirring until smooth. Remove from heat; stir in cream. Pour into crust; chill for a few minutes. In a bowl, beat together cream cheese, icing sugar, milk and vanilla until smooth. Spread over chocolate; chill a few minutes.

3. Before serving, decorate with strawberries and kiwi fruit. In a small saucepan, melt jelly; brush over flan. Garnish with almonds and dust with sifted icing sugar.

Cream Cheese-Filled Brownies

MAKES 12 TO 16 BROWNIES

PREHEAT OVEN TO 350° F (180° C)
8-INCH (2 L) SQUARE BAKING DISH SPRAYED WITH VEGETABLE SPRAY

Filling

4 oz	light cream cheese, softened	125 g
2 tbsp	granulated sugar	25 mL
2 tbsp	2% milk	25 mL
1 tsp	vanilla extract	5 mL

Cake

1 cup	packed brown sugar	250 mL
1/3 cup	light sour cream	75 mL
1/4 cup	vegetable oil	50 mL
1	egg	1
1	egg white	1
3/4 cup	all-purpose flour	175 mL
1/2 cup	cocoa	125 mL
1 tsp	baking powder	5 mL

1. Make the filling: In a Batter Bowl with an electric mixer, beat together cream cheese, sugar, milk and vanilla until smooth. Set aside.

2. Make the cake: In a Thatsa® Bowl, whisk together brown sugar, sour cream, oil, whole egg and egg white. In a separate bowl, stir together flour, cocoa and baking powder. Add liquid ingredients to dry, blending just until mixed.

3. Pour half the cake batter into prepared pan. Spoon filling on top; spread with a Sandwich Spreader. Pour remaining batter into pan. Bake 20 to 25 minutes or until just barely loose at center.

Lemon and Lime Meringue Pie

SERVES 12

PREHEAT OVEN TO 375° F (190° C)
8- OR 8.5-INCH (2 OR 2.25 L) SPRINGFORM PAN SPRAYED WITH
VEGETABLE SPRAY

Crust

1 cup	all-purpose flour	250 mL
1/3 cup	granulated sugar	75 mL
1/3 cup	cold margarine *or* butter	75 mL
2 tbsp	2% yogurt	25 mL
1 to 2 tbsp	cold water	15 to 25 mL

Filling

1/4 cup	freshly squeezed lime juice	50 mL
1/4 cup	freshly squeezed lemon juice	50 mL
1 1/2 tsp	grated lime zest (about 2 limes)	7 mL
1 1/2 tsp	grated lemon zest (about 1 lemon)	7 mL
1	egg	1
1	egg white	1
1 1/3 cups	granulated sugar	325 mL
1 1/4 cups	water	300 mL
1/3 cup	cornstarch	75 mL
2 tsp	margarine *or* butter	10 mL

Topping

3	egg whites	3
1/2 tsp	cream of tartar	2 mL
1/3 cup	granulated sugar	75 mL

1. In a Thatsa® Bowl, combine flour and sugar; cut in margarine just until crumbly. With a Tupperific Spatula, gradually stir in yogurt and just enough of the cold water so dough comes together. Pat onto bottom and sides of pan. Bake approximately 18 minutes or until light brown. Raise heat to 425° F (220° C).

2. Meanwhile, in a Thatsa® Bowl Jr., combine lime and lemon juices, lime and lemon zest, egg and egg white; set aside.

3. In saucepan combine sugar, water and cornstarch. Bring to a boil; reduce heat to low and simmer for approximately 1 minute, stirring constantly, until mixture is smooth and thick. Pour a bit of the cornstarch mixture into the lemon-lime mixture and whisk together. Pour all back into saucepan and simmer, stirring constantly, for 5 minutes, or until thickened and smooth. Remove from heat. Stir in margarine. Pour into crust.

4. In a Batter Bowl, beat egg whites with cream of tartar until foamy; continue to beat, gradually adding sugar. Beat until stiff peaks form. Spread over filling. Bake approximately 5 minutes or until golden brown. Let cool.

Chocolate Pecan Pie

SERVES 8

PREHEAT OVEN TO 350° F (180° C)
9- TO 10-INCH (23 TO 25 CM) FLAN PAN WITH REMOVABLE BOTTOM,
BUTTERED

Crust

1 1/2 cups	all-purpose flour	375 mL
1/3 cup	icing sugar	75 mL
3/4 cup	butter	175 mL

Filling

3 oz	semi-sweet chocolate	90 g
2 tbsp	butter	25 mL
1 cup	corn syrup	250 mL
1 cup	granulated sugar	250 mL
3	eggs	3
1 cup	pecan halves	250 mL
1/4 cup	miniature chocolate chips (optional)	50 mL

1. Make the crust: In a Thatsa® Bowl stir together flour and icing sugar. With a pastry cutter or two knives, cut in butter until dough forms. Form into a ball. Pat into bottom and sides of flan pan. Bake 15 to 20 minutes or until golden. Cool in pan on wire rack.

2. Make the filling: In a Thatsa® Bowl Jr., melt the chocolate with butter over hot (not boiling) water, stirring until smooth; set aside. In a saucepan, heat corn syrup with sugar until liquid; remove from heat and beat into chocolate mixture. Using a Tupperific Spatula, stir in pecans and, if desired, chocolate chips. Pour into crust. Bake about 45 minutes or until slightly loose just at center. Cool on wire rack.

Tropical Fruit Tart

SERVES 12

PREHEAT OVEN TO 400° F (200° C)
9-INCH (2 L) TART OR SPRINGFORM PAN
SPRAYED WITH VEGETABLE SPRAY

1 3/4 cups	2% yogurt	425 mL
2/3 cup	granulated sugar	150 mL
1/2 cup	light sour cream	125 mL
3 tbsp	frozen orange juice concentrate, thawed	45 mL
2 tbsp	all-purpose flour	25 mL
1 1/2 tsp	orange zest	7 mL
Crust		
1 1/4 cups	all-purpose flour	300 mL
1/4 cup	icing sugar	50 mL
1/3 cup	margarine	75 mL
3 tbsp	cold water (approximate)	45 mL
Topping		
3 cups	sliced fruit (kiwi fruit, mangos, papayas, star fruit)	750 mL

1. Crust: In a Thatsa® Bowl combine flour with sugar; cut in margarine until crumbly. With a Tupperific Spatula, gradually stir in water, adding 1 tbsp (15 mL) more if necessary to make dough hold together. Pat into pan and bake for 15 minutes or until browned. Reduce heat to 375° F (190° C).

2. Meanwhile, in a Thatsa® Bowl Jr., combine yogurt, sugar, sour cream, orange juice concentrate, flour and orange zest; mix well and pour over crust. Bake for 35 to 45 minutes or until filling is set. Let cool and refrigerate until chilled.

3. Topping: Decoratively arrange sliced fruit over filling.

A

Apple pecan streusel cake, 29

B

Banana chocolate chip muffins, 6
Banana spice muffins, 9
Bars, granola, 18
Biscotti, 24
Blueberry cornmeal muffins, 8
Bran muffins, 10
Brownies, 41

C

Cakes:
  apple pecan streusel, 29
  carrot, 30-31
  espresso chocolate, 36
  strawberry cream, 27-28
Carrot cake, 30-31
Carrot-raisin muffins, 7
Cheesecake:
  chocolate, 33
  marble mocha, 34
Chocolate:
  cake, 36
  cheesecake, 33
  cookies, 23
  pecan pie, 44
  strawberry kiwi flan, 38-39
Chocolate chips:
  banana muffins, 6
  peanut butter cookies, 20
Cookies, 12-24
  chocolate chunk, 23
  gingersnaps, 16-17
  lemon sugar, 14
  oatmeal date, 21
  peanut butter, 20
  pecan biscotti, 24
  shortbread, 12
Cornmeal, blueberry muffins, 8
Cream cake, strawberry, 27-28

Cream cheese:
  brownies filled with, 41
  chocolate flan, 38-39
  frosting, 30-31

F

Flan, cream cheese chocolate, 38-39
Frosting, cream cheese, 30-31
Fruit tart, 46

G

Gingersnaps, 16-17
Granola bars, 18

L

Lemon and lime meringue pie, 42-43
Lemon sugar cookies, 14

M

Marble mocha cheesecake, 34
Muffins, 6-10
  banana chocolate chip, 6
  banana spice, 9
  blueberry cornmeal, 8
  bran, 10
  carrot-raisin, 7

O

Oatmeal date cookies, 21

P

Peanut butter cookies, 20
Pecan biscotti, 24
Pecan chocolate pie, 44
Pie, *See also* Tart
  chocolate pecan, 44
  lemon and lime meringue, 42-43

S

Shortbread, 12
Sour cream topping, 33
Strawberry cream cake, 27-28
Strawberry cream cheese flan, 38-39
Streusel cake, 29
Sugar cookies, 14

T

Tart, tropical fruit, 46. *See also* Pie
Toppings, sour cream, 32

The Tupperware Opportunity has all the ingredients to make your dreams come true!

- Earn money based on **your** efforts
- Have a schedule that works with **your** family
- Be recognized for doing a good job
- Be rewarded with wonderful gifts and trips
- Earn your own van!

What ever the mix, **you** can take control of **your** career and income! Why not take the first step toward making your dreams come true...ask your Consultant about the Tupperware Opportunity today!

Your Tupperware Consultant

You can also reach your local Tupperware Distributor listed in the white pages of your telephone directory under Tupperware, or call Tupperware Canada at 1-800-567-0400.